Habit Stacking Project

7 Steps To Build Easy, Effective and Everlasting Habits

by Tyler Coleman

Table of Contents

Disclaimer

While all attempts have been made to verify the information provided in this book, the author does not assume any responsibility for errors, omissions, or contrary interpretations of the subject matter contained within. The information provided in this book is for educational and entertainment purposes only. The reader is responsible for his or her own actions and the author does not accept any responsibilities for any liabilities or damages, real or perceived, resulting from the use of this information.

Introduction

Most people would agree that they do not have time to indulge in things they want to do because their time is tied up with things they have to do. This is true for a lot of people, but there are ways to change this.

Many of us go through our days following routines, these routines are the way we divide our time to make sure we get to everything we need to do. These routines probably began as new responsibilities were added to our lives, and we adopted these routines out of necessity.

The good news is…we don't have to follow these routines out of necessity, there are ways to do both, what we want and what we need to do.

Habit stacking has been around for a while now and it is not about to go anywhere anytime soon, because when something really works, it sticks around. Habits are not always bad, although we tend to equate habits with bad behavior, they are also associated with positive behaviors.

Flipping the switch and acquiring beneficial habits is a pretty easy thing to do; if you know a bit about "habits" and human behavior.

You will be shocked at how simple it is to foster positive habits and you don't have to spend time eliminating any of your bad habits either. As you progress through the 7 steps to habit stacking, your negative habits will begin to give way to your positive habits.

Sometimes focusing on what is going right will produce a better outcome than focusing on what is wrong.

Habit stacking is something you already do and you probably don't even realize it because you don't recognize it as habit stacking. If you always wash the dishes after you eat and then relax with a cup of coffee, you are guilty of habit stacking. There are too many stacks to list them all in one book, but you get the idea.

As you read through the book and tackle the 7 steps, you will be amazed at how easy it is to change your habits/routine to suit your goals. Everyone has goals, of course getting from point A to point B is always a matter of personal preference.

Making choices that compliment your goals and make the trip from point A to B easier and more enjoyable is what this book is all about.

Sometimes it's not about how much you can do, but the quality of what you do that matters most. Filling our days with routines and tasks that take but never give, can really take a toll on our well-being.

Creating new habits that give back, even if it is just 10 minutes of relaxing or taking a walk, can create a cycle of changes, or a stack of habits that will really change life for the better.

Chapter 1 – Behavioral Psychology and Habits

Behavioral psychology is where all of this habit stacking first came about. Behavioral psychology is the study of how our minds and behaviors connect. Researchers in the field of behavioral psychology study why people behave the way they do and this research is concerned with identifying patterns in actions and behaviors.

Researchers from Oxford University discovered something amazing in 2007; newborn babies have more neurons that the average adult, 41% more to be exact. This new realization led to more research and study into how we learn and the importance of neurons in that learning process.

A large number of neurons are used when we begin learning; these neurons allow us to learn lots of different things. As we begin to narrow down our learning and start to develop specific skills and ignore other skills, the number of neurons changes.

Neurons strengthen connections in the brain, they group together to strengthen connections we use most often and they disappear from connections we do not use.

Babies are learning everything, they need lots of neurons to make the connections for social interaction so they can interact with the world around them and this requires a large number of neurons. As they begin to develop skills and ignore others, the number of neurons change. Waste not want not.

This research can tell us a lot about habits. Habits are actions and behaviors we engage in regularly. Anything we do regularly is strengthened with stronger and stronger neuron connections, the actions/behaviors we don't engage in don't require any connections.

You change the neuron connections in your brain when you develop habits. This is called synaptic pruning.

The brain creates a network of neurons to support your daily habits; these networks become stronger the more we repeat these habits. Tapping into this built in ability will help you change current habits and create new ones.

Once you begin to repeat the new habits, the brain redirects neurons to strengthen the new connections and depletes the neuron network used to strengthen old habits.

Replacing old with new becomes easier and easier the more you repeat the activity.

What is a Habit and Why Are They Hard to Change?

We have already covered neuron involvement in habit creation, but there is more to the puzzle than the strength of neuron networks. Changing a habit is much harder than stacking a new one into existing habits.

Change requires an understanding of how habits are formed, and behavioral psychology explains this rather neatly.

Habits are actions or behaviors that follow three simple rules; Reminder, Routine, and Reward. The reminder triggers the routine and the routine delivers a reward.

When your alarm clock goes off in the morning it Reminds you to begin a routine, the routine is preparing yourself for the day, the reward can be money from your job, or any other benefit you gain from getting out of bed and preparing for the day.

The reminder can be anything that triggers you to perform a routine that results in a reward.

Changing habits is harder than adding new ones because you already strengthened the neuron network, the Reminder will always exist and the routine will result in a reward.

Adding to this provides a quick reward if you can make the habit stick, but changing the habit is hard because it takes time for a brand new habit to strengthen the network and it takes repetition over time to recognize the new reminder, perform the new routine, and receive a new reward.

It is actually more rewarding for us to fall back on old habits and get that quick reward.

Why does Habit Stacking Work?

Habit stacking works because you are adding new habits by attaching them to habits that already have strong neuron connections and proven rewards. Even though you are creating an entirely new habit, attaching it to an old habit using

habit stacking will help the habit stick.

The Reminder for the habit stack remains the same but it now reminds you to perform an additional routine while still performing the old routine, the old reward is still there but another reward is added to it, it does not replace the old reward.

One of the easiest ways to build new habits is to stack them. Habit stacking is all about stacking new habits onto old habits that already have strong neuron connections in the brain.

Habit stacking helps you create strong new habits by plugging them into the network that already exists.

Here are a few examples of habit stacking:

- After I eat my lunch I will spend two minutes meditating

- Before I have my morning coffee I will make the bed

These two examples show how you can plug in new habits by attaching them to existing habits. Lunch is an existing habit, by adding the statement, I will spend two minutes meditating, you are creating a new habit that is triggered by an old one!

Pretty easy stuff, but it does require a bit of commitment on your part. You must actually engage in the action/behavior if you want it to stick.

Now you have some background on how the brain uses neurons to support habits. This information is about all you need to understand the concept of habit stacking.

You can create any new habit you want and help it take hold by stacking it on top of old habits.

You can even string a few of them together to get maximum results with minimal effort. It is easier to strengthen existing connections than it is to create brand new ones.

Chapter 2 – 7 Steps to for Creating Positive Habits

Using the precepts of behavioral psychology as a guide, these 7 steps will take you from wanting to make a change to creating new positive habits. These steps will provide the ground work for positive change and making it stick.

Before you actually create your own habit stacking project using these steps, it is important to understand the psychology behind why change is not always permanent.

In chapter 1 we took a look at why habits are hard to change. There is another side to the coin, sometimes it is easy to get started with a change but difficult to follow through.

Creating a habit is done in stages and according to research by the European Journal of Psychology, it takes at least 66 days before changes become automatic, and it can take up to 200 or more days before those changes become habits.

There are solid reasons why it takes so long for new behaviors to become habits. Remember, creating new habits is different from stacking habits. Creating new habits takes time and a good perspective on why many attempts to create new habits eventually fail.

We have all made new year's resolutions and ended up watching those resolutions go up in smoke. Why is this information important? Because if you have a realistic understanding of how and why, you won't feel defeated when weeks turn into months; it is all about keeping you motivated.

Motivation is a key factor in why actions and behavioral changes fail. This list of reasons why changes fail will help you see the reality of what you are about to do, and how to stay away from misconceptions that can undermine your motivation.

- We like to do as much as we can all at once to effect change and more/bigger is always better

- Big changes take time and become overwhelming, this leads to frustration and failure

- Focusing on the reward/outcome more than the actual change itself

- We don't think small wins are worth as much as big ones, small changes are not as attractive as conquering large changes so we always go for the big change

These misconceptions mean that close to 81% of all changes will fail. This news sounds like a motivation killer but it is not. Motivation will only lead to failure if it is unrealistic.

If you motivate yourself with the promise of a big reward for big change, that motivation will wane when the change and reward takes too long to happen.

Motivation itself is not static, it does not stay the same from the beginning to the end of changing a habit; it doesn't even stay the same from the beginning to the end of a single day.

Motivation ebbs like a tide, one moment it is high, the next it is almost non-existent. This brings us to the first of the 7 steps for creating positive habits.

1. Motivation – Motivation fails quickly when results are not seen fast enough. Your motivation should not be about making a huge change and reaping the rewards quickly.

You motivation should focus on change itself, any change is positive movement in the right direction. Motivation should be about moving forward, even if you do so in tiny increments.

2. Start Very Small – Small changes are easier to make and easier to maintain. The longer you maintain a change, no matter how small that change is,the more likely it is to stick and become a habit.

3. Break Big Changes into Smaller Ones – If you begin and realize your change is too big to handle, break it down into smaller changes and conquer the smaller ones until you have conquered the big one.

4. Increase Slowly – If you find that you are making a small change with ease, resist the urge to leap forward. Go slow and steady.

5. Don't Increase if You Cannot Maintain – If you are having trouble keeping up with the small changes you

have made do not increase at all until you can maintain your small changes.

6. Mistakes Happen Don't Give Up – Mistakes and slip ups happen, life happens, get back on track as quickly as you can. Do not let setbacks turn into failures, they are only setbacks and they do not have to ruin all the work you have put into your change.

7. Keep Track of Your Victories No Matter How Small – Pat yourself on the back for every victory. Each month you stay the course is another month closer to creating those positive habits you are working toward. As long as you don't give up, change will happen, no matter how long it takes.

These 7 steps may not seem like much but they are. Each step will keep you moving forward and forward is always positive.

Each step can help you maintain motivation, and each step will help you overcome any pitfalls you encounter. Moving forward is the key to success.

As you read about habit stacking apply these principles as you work toward those positive changes. If you stay focused and do not give up, you will achieve the changes you are after.

Habit stacking will make it easy for you to add changes, and these steps will help you maintain them.

The more familiar you become with habit stacking and the changes it helps you create, you will begin to realize how important these steps are. There will be times when you won't want to do it, life will get in the way, and you will slip up; these 7 steps will help you see that slip up for what it is...just a bump in the road.

These steps will not change how you think or give you super powers, they will just keep you focused on the reality of what you are doing.

Sometimes we get caught up in events that happened during the day and we have to deal. Just because your life gets a little out of control now and then does not mean you have to give up on what something you want.

If you want to quit smoking, don't give up on that desire, keep making small changes and working your way toward the ultimate goal. Each time you reach for a piece of nicotine gum you gain a victory.

If you want to get a better job and you need another degree to do it, start taking online classes. It doesn't matter how long it takes you to get that new degree, keep your focus on each victory; every course you pass brings you closer to your goal. Eventually you will have that degree and that new job because you didn't give up.

No system is perfect and this system is meant to help you get where you are going. It is not a formula for success, it is a formula for revealing your potential.

As your behavior and actions change, you will change too; your self-esteem will grow and so will your confidence.

Chapter 3 – A Simple Mini-Habit Stacking Project

Mini habits are short, simple additions to your existing routine. The concept behind mini habit stacking is to use the existing connections in your brain to help you make new short simple habits.

Starting with simple mini habit stacking projects will also produce new connections that will strengthen each time you decide to stack a habit.

Small, simple additions are easier to stick to when you first add them. It takes time to add big additions because there are many reasons you may not be able to engage in the action or behavior.

Each time you don't perform the action or behavior, the longer it will take to stack the new habit.

In order to stack new habits and make them stick, you need to repeat the action or behavior. Small and simple changes and additions will work best when you first start to create new habits.

Small, steady, steps in the right direction will build up those networks of neurons and soon you will be amazed at how much you have changed your daily routine.

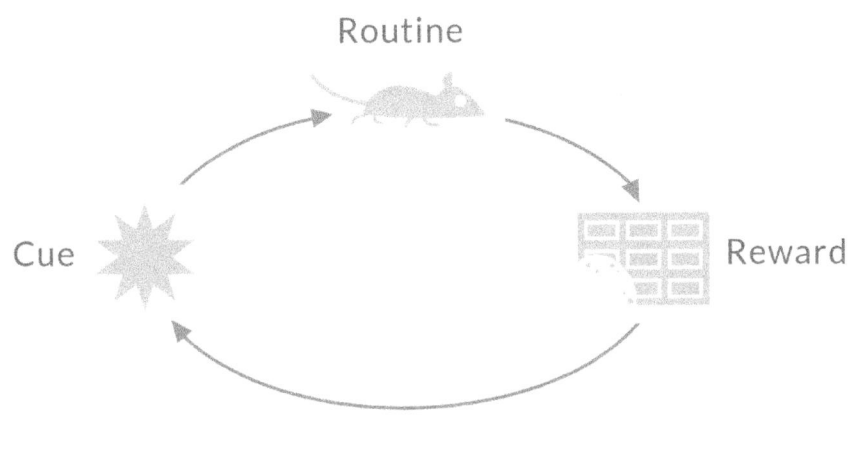

Routine

Cue

Reward

THE HABIT LOOP

The first step in this mini habit stacking project is to come up with two new additions you would like to make to your daily routine. Remember, they will be small at first and simple to add; they should not require a lot of preparation or a big change to your existing routine.

 Think about things you would like to do every day, for instance, you may want to add stretching to your morning routine, or learn some Italian before your trip to Italy. Both of these can be part of your simple mini habit stacking project.

Here is an example of how a simple mini habit stacking project works:

- Make a list of all the activities and behaviors in your daily routine

- Make a list of additions you would like to make to your daily routine

- Choose two additions from your list and find a good place to stack them in your daily routine

- You decide to add stretching to your morning routine, and learning Italian to your afternoon routine

- Tell yourself – I am going to do stretches for two minutes before I have my morning coffee

- Tell yourself – I am going to listen to my Italian language CD for two minutes after I eat my lunch

- Your existing routine in the morning will now include two minutes of stretching before you have your coffee, and your afternoon routine will now include two minutes of language CD's after you eat your lunch

Even though it is tempting to add more time for your new additions you have to resist. The point is to add these new actions and behaviors to the habits you already have; making them longer leaves more room for other things to creep in and ruin your new habits.

Everyone can carve out two, two minute intervals during their day, even busy people can stick to two minutes twice a day.

Each time you successfully stack the new mini habit, the stronger that habit will become. Soon they will be a part of your daily routine and you won't find yourself thinking about them.

You will just do them as part of your day, once this happens, you can begin to change how long you will do each new mini habit.

Remember, stick to the two-minute time frame and do not add more than two new mini habits. Once you have conquered this mini habit stacking project, you will be ready to add more time or more habits.

The important part is to learn how to strengthen those neuron connections. Moving on to bigger and better will happen but there is no reason to force it.

Forcing longer time commitments or too many new habits will just confuse the entire process. For instance: If you are late for work, two minutes will not make much of a difference; but if you are trying to add 5 or more minutes, you will have to let it go so you can get to work.

Short time intervals ensure that you will be able follow through on your new mini habits.

Mini Habit Stacking and Bad Habits

A simple mini habit stacking project can also help you break bad habits. If you smoke, you can try simple mini habit stacking to break the hold that bad habit has on your time, actions, and behaviors.

You don't need to quit smoking when you begin this project, it is about making small changes that will become habits; and eventually these new habits will help you quit.

Mini habit stacking is best for this because the habits that accompany smoking, or trigger smoking are small/mini habits such as, lighting up while you drink coffee, smoking before you get in the car, having a cigarette while waiting for the bus. These types of habit connections are perfect for inserting mini habits

Make a list of the habits that accompany the smoking habit or any bad habit you want to change. For instance, if you light up a smoke every time you have a cup of coffee, you can add a new habit between the coffee and the cigarette so that drinking coffee becomes a reminder for performing a new routine.

This extra habit will weaken the original connection/reminder between coffee and smoking.

Don't tell yourself you are quitting, and don't think about not smoking; put the emphasis on the new habit you are going to do when you have a cup of coffee. You are breaking the connection between smoking and drinking coffee; that is all you are doing when you first begin this project.

Maybe you can add a habit like, *while I have my coffee I will check my messages,* or, *when I have my coffee I will play solitaire on my phone.*

Whatever you decide to do when you have coffee, make sure you enjoy it, you want the new behavior to have a clear reward; checking messages has a clear reward, you find out what others want to tell you.

You want this habit to replace smoking while drinking coffee, it is not meant to replace smoking completely so there is no stress when you first begin.

Once you have added this new habit and you don't smoke with coffee, it is time to stack another mini habit. Scrutinize your day, and find another strong habit that is stacked with smoking.

Maybe you always light up as soon as you leave work. Now you will stack a mini habit between leaving work and lighting up. Once this new habit is stacked between leaving work and smoking, move on to another habit stack and add another mini habit.

Now that you have weakened the habit stacks that accompany your smoking, it will be easier to start a program to quit. The reason this will make it easier for you to follow a quitting program is because you will be dealing only with the smoking habit, not the stacked habits and reminders that accompany your smoking.

This mini stacking project can work for many bad habits as well as creating good ones. As you weaken old connections and strengthen new ones, changing the bad ones become easier.

Any habit is hard to break, good and bad, and the more habits you have stacked with your bad habits, the more reminders that bad habit has!

Chapter 4 – Creating a Lifestyle Habit Stacking Project

Now that you know how to make changes and maintain them using the 7 steps and mini habit stacking principles, you can begin to make changes to your life style as well as your daily routine.

Your daily routine includes all of the mini habits you have added, and now it's time to create a personal habit stacking project that will help you overhaul your life style.

Make a list of lifestyle changes you would like to make. Include everything you want to do no matter how overwhelming they may seem.

Now make a list of daily habits you already have, including the ones you added using mini habit stacking. Next to the items in your daily habits list, add the lifestyle changes that mesh with the habits already in your list.

For instance: If you have already used mini habit stacking to add stretches to your morning routine, taking the stairs after lunch to your afternoon routine, and meditating to your evening routine, and one of the lifestyle changes you have listed is to lose weight; you can put lose weight next to your morning stretches, next to taking the stairs after lunch, and next to meditating in the evening.

Once you have your lifestyle/daily routine list complete, it's time to figure out how you can begin making those lifestyle changes using the mini habits you have already added.

These new changes will be small too, but they will have the potential to change your lifestyle when they become daily habits.

Let's focus on the lose weight; add small changes to each routine you have already made changes to.

Your new daily routine may end up looking something like this:

- I do morning stretches before having my morning coffee, and *take a short walk before taking my shower*

- *I walk to the park to eat my lunch,* then take the stairs instead of the elevator when I return to work after lunch

- *I take a short walk after dinner,* then I meditate for a few minutes before I turn in for the evening

This list is not yours, of course your list will have your habits and changes listed, it is meant to give you an idea of what you are trying to accomplish with your lifestyle habit stacking project.

This list shows how small changes can become changes to your lifestyle and help you create positive habits that will help you attain your goal.

Losing weight does not have to be done within a given time limit. Actually the reality is, if you stay slow and steady, you will lose weight.

When you add changes to your routine that involve moving more, your weight will go down; slowly, but it will go down and it will be more of a permanent weight loss.

Losing weight is only one example of a lifestyle change and the addition of a bit more physical movement is only one way to make a positive change. You may also want to change the way you eat; creating a healthy diet one food at a time will be easier to maintain than changing everything you eat at once.

 For instance:

- I do morning stretches before having my coffee and *I include some healthy grains in my breakfast*

- *I eat a health bar instead of cookies for lunch* then I take the stairs instead of the elevator when I return to work from lunch

- *Instead of a snack after dinner, I relax in a warm bath,* then I meditate before turning in

There are a multitude of ways you can use small changes to make big changes in your lifestyle.

If you were to make these small changes, your lifestyle would be healthier all around, and you wouldn't need to work out like mad at the gym until you give up either.

Small, steady, stacks can create awesome lifestyle habits that will deliver what you want and those changes will be permanent if you follow the steps and learn to stack those habits.

Try using the 7 steps for creating positive habits, and habit stacking to make permanent changes to your life. Keep it simple, try out different habit stacking until you hit on the ones that are perfect for you.

There is no reason to rush or demand immediate change; slow and steady really does win the race because you will learn to pace yourself and recognize the new positive changes as they happen.

You can make as many lists and stacks as you want until you learn what works for you. Everyone is different, it may take some trial and error before you find your perfect fit.

Don't give up, just keep trying out new stacks until you can maintain, and once you maintain, you can add more; the combinations are endless, and so is your potential!

Make your objectives S.M.A.R.T.

The acronym S.M.A.R.T. implies Specific, Measurable, Attainable, Realistic and Time-sensitive.

Specific:

Objectives are no spot to waffle. They are no spot to be dubious. Equivocal objectives produce vague results. Deficient objectives produce inadequate fates.

Quantifiable:

Continuously set objectives that are quantifiable. I would say "specifically quantifiable" to consider our guideline of being specific.

Achievable:

One of the impeding things that many individuals benefit—with aims—is setting objectives that are high to the point that they are unattainable.

Realistic:

The root expression of realistic is "real." An objective must be something that we can sensibly make "real" or a "reality" in our lives. There are some objectives that are just not realistic.

You must have the capacity to say, regardless of the possibility that it is a hugely stretching objective, that yes, in fact, it is totally realistic—that you could make it.

Time:

Each objective ought to have a timeframe attached to it. One of the effective parts of an extraordinary objective is that it has an end—a time in which you are shooting to achieve it.

As time passes by, you chip away at it since you would prefer not to get behind, and you work constantly on the grounds that you need to meet the due date.

You might even need to separate a major objective into different parts of estimation and timeframes—that is OK.

Set littler objectives and work them out time permitting. A S.M.A.R.T. objective has a timeline.

Conclusion

When you started this book you knew you wanted to make positive changes in your life. You knew you wanted to look better, feel better, work better, or just be happier. Now you have some new information and skills to help you make real changes instead of setting yourself up for disappointment.

Each new stack of habits you have created have changed your life for the better. It is amazing how much time you can squeeze out of a day if you don't overload every moment.

Many times it is just a matter of realizing lots of small changes equal big changes when they are all stacked together.

Your entire day is a series of reminders, routines, and rewards, and now you have the tools you need to create the reminders and routines that provide you with the rewards you really want.

As you create new habits and make lifestyle changes you will realize that once they are maintained long enough, you can create new ones. Habits are just behaviors and actions that help us get from point A to B, they are nothing more and nothing less.

Don't worry about failure, just keep moving forward and you will eventually have the life you want and deserve.